ACQUAINTED

WITH

THE NIGHT

EDITED BY LISA RUSS SPAAR

ACQUAINTED
INSOMNIA
WITH
POEMS
THE NIGHT

COLUMBIA UNIVERSITY PRESS

NEW YORK

COLUMBIA UNIVERSITY PRESS

Publishers Since 1893

New York   Chichester, West Sussex

Copyright © 1999 by Columbia University Press

Library of Congress Cataloging-in-Publication Data

Acquainted with the night : Insomnia poems / edited by Lisa Russ Spaar.

p. cm.   Includes index.

ISBN 0–231–11544–x (cloth : alk. paper)

1. Insomnia Poetry.   2. Night—Poetry.   3. Sleep—Poetry.

I. Spaar, Lisa Russ.

PN6110.I56I57   1999

808.81'9353—DC21   99–20099

∞

Casebound editions of Columbia University Press
books are printed on permanent and durable acid-free paper.

Printed in the United States of America

Designed by Linda Secondari

Illustrations by Martha Lewis

c 10 9 8 7 6 5 4 3 2

To Pete

Lie in the arms of nightlong fire,
To celebrate the waking, wake.

—Muriel Rukeyser

Contents

Acknowledgments

For their many kindnesses in matters both aesthetic and practical, I am deeply grateful to Sydney Blair, George Garrett, Ted Genoways, Debra Nystrom, Greg and Trisha Orr, James Raimes, Mark Saunders, Charles Simic, and Charles Wright.

For his adventurous, generous spirit in suggesting and locating poems, I thank the tireless Stephen Margulies, who has contributed invaluably to this anthology.

For their help in dating poems and in preparing the manuscript and biographies, I owe a great debt to Lara Glenum, my colleagues at the University of Virginia, Wayne Ray, and, especially, Deborah Slicer.

For their insistence, patience, and humor, which both protracted and enriched this project, I must thank my three children, Jocelyn, Adam, and Suzannah.

When you're lying awake with a dismal headache,
and repose is taboo'd by anxiety,
I conceive you may use any language you choose
to indulge in, without impropriety . . .

—*W. S. Gilbert, from* Iolanthe

And soon all of us will sleep under the earth, we
who never let each other sleep above it.

—*Marina Tsvetaeva, from "I Know the Truth"*

ACQUAINTED

WITH

THE NIGHT

The experts say that most of us will suffer a bout of sleep-lessness at least once in our lifetimes, an irksome spate of waking nocturnal hours related to personal crisis, worry, grief, or passion—or even a particularly potent espresso imbibed too late in the evening, or a bit of bad beef. But many people—a third of the population, at least—endure sleep disorders that are chronic and debilitating. Insomnia is not a new problem, either: the Hittites, ancient Greeks and Romans, and medieval Europeans all recorded cures for sleeplessness, ranging from a night spent in the temple of one's favorite god to sleep potions concocted from man-drake and lettuce juice to special talismanic bedside candles made from mummified hands. Little wonder, then, that poets both ancient and modern have made insomnia the subject of innumerable poems. A fretful night of tossing and turning can become, in the hands of Sappho or Tu Fu, Mirabai or Gerard Manley Hopkins, a visionary, sexual, or artistic experience—a crisis of good or of evil, a dark night of the soul that may either bless or curse, that can lead in some cases to epiphany and in others to confrontation with chaos or Death itself, the "big sleep" that insomnia so often attempts to ward off. Whether staking artistic claims on the metaphysical turf of sleeplessness or succumbing to its relentless somatic and psychic reclamations, the poets gathered in this anthology reveal, tacitly or explicitly, that something about the insomniacal experience is directly related to why they make poems. As Whitman points out, "night, sleep, death and the stars" are the themes a poet's soul loves best.

Solitude and Vigil

Vladimir Nabokov, a famous insomniac, called sleep "the most moronic fraternity in the world, with the heaviest dues and the crudest rituals . . . [a] nightly betrayal of reason, humanity, genius." For Nabokov and others like him, the wrench of parting with consciousness was almost unbearable, an obliteration of essential imaginary faculties, with Somnus "that black-masked headsman binding [him] to the block." Like other notorious literary insomniacs—Marcel Proust, Charles Dickens, Elizabeth Bishop, Yannis Ritsos—Nabokov wanted, literally and artistically, to be an eye awake—a seer—in a sleeping world, a solitary watcher among the unconscious. The word *watch* derives from the Old English *wæccan*, to be or stay awake, to keep vigil, and in many of these poems, the speaker, eyes open, is a lone keeper of awareness. Abandoned by sleep, and by those who have surrendered to its oblivion, these poets find themselves

engaged and identified by insomnia—and sometimes even
more than a little proud of their wretched wakefulness.

The poet awake while others sleep confronts his or her
loneliness in a world askew, with an intensified, at times
almost hallucinatory visual and aural acuity. An interior,
fun-house array of mirrors furnishes many of these
poems, as their wakeful speakers search rooms and win-
dows and looking glasses for some remnant of another, or
of a self. *Who am I?* Elizabeth Bishop seems to be asking in
"Insomnia," and, perhaps more urgently, *Where are you?*, as
she lies awake in

. . . that world inverted
where left is always right,
where the shadows are really the body,
where we stay awake all night,
where the heavens are shallow as the sea
is now deep, and you love me.

The betrayals Bishop hints at are personal as well as
physical—the poem's narrator feels bereft of more than
sleep—but it is the isolating, bodily fact of insomnia that
carries the poem to that realization. We see this again and
again in the first section of the book—poems in which the
wakeful, often with a dose of black humor and horror, con-
front through their insomnia

4   The company of a blank wall,
     The company of time and eternity

     Which, begging your pardon,
     Cast no image
     As they admire themselves in the mirror,
     While you stand to the side
     Pulling a hanky out
     To wipe your brow surreptitiously.

(*Charles Simic, "Mirrors at 4 A.M."*)

The experience can be existential and utterly isolating. What happens, these poets seem to be asking, when you alone are awake and you look into your bathroom mirror, into yourself, and, as Joyce Carol Oates says, "there's nothing/beyond the surface not even/you"?

Noises, too, assert themselves on the nocturnally wakeful with new, exaggerated meanings while the rest of the world is asleep: the voices, as Dana Gioia writes, that "have escaped you until now,/the venting furnace, the floorboards underfoot,/the steady accusations of the clock/numbering the minutes no one will mark." Sometimes it's Melissa Kirsch's "gamelan" of street cacophony, or Alexander Pushkin's "old wives' chatter of fate," or Cornelius Eady's birds, "Jeering as only/The well-rested can"; at other times it is a black, sea-like silence that "roars like a speech/and thunders up the bed," a deafening ocean of utter loneliness that Osip Mandelstam and others—Gregory Orr, Jane Kenyon, and Cao Bá Quát—try to ride out by reading late into the night. Beneath the edgy music of Sylvia Plath's "Insomniac" is the seething hive of her own driven sense of genius and doom. But it's not all a dire din. Herman Melville, in his wonderful poem on insomnia and Flemish art, lulls himself with drowsy musings on Teniers's dark and peaceful painting in "The Bench of Boors," and Donald Justice's Tremayne "really likes the little hum,/Which is the last sound of all nightsounds to decay"—the "faint, celestial surf" of "pure inbetweenness," that is both solipsistic and a nod to the world beyond the self that goes on despite our bodies and our willful or helpless watching. Insomnia, it would seem, by virtue or curse of its inherently isolating nature, is for many both a physical and a metaphysical condition.

For some poets, the loneliness of insomnia is narcissistic, bodily, and interior, but others who keep watch at night are perambulators, wanderers of the sleeping world—Whitman, for example, with his pantheistic and empathetic pilgrimages, "stepping/and stopping,/Bending with open eyes over the shut eyes of sleepers"; or Frost's dark, wordless acquaintance with the night; or the regnant power and desolation of Shakespeare's Henry IV as he walks among his sleeping men. But whether the vigil being kept is private or public, the insomniacs in these poems come face to face with an aloneness that precedes and supersedes any episode of sleeplessness. "When [poets] wake it becomes night, and they become alone, they alone are awake," writes W. S. Merwin. Sleepless in a sleeping world, the poet/insomniac embodies the hunch that consciousness means confronting ultimate solitude, and this special awareness can be addictive even as it irritates, frightens, and surprises. In "Psalm: The New Day," Mark Jarman acknowledges that it is, perhaps, his role as poet/insomniac to work the borders between sleep and waking, to keep watch over the often "ugly confrontation" between "nightmare's many mansions" and "the new day, the day's newness":

A bad night lies ahead
 And a new day beyond that—
A simple sequence, but hard
 To remember in the right order.

Anguish and Longing

The poet with eyes open at night learns not only what it means to keep a solitary vigil but also what it means, or might mean, to be asleep: to surrender, to lose that light by which we make our way, to die. In "Aubade" Philip Larkin writes,

Waking at four to soundless dark, I stare.
In time the curtain-edges will grow light.
Till then I see what's really always there:
Unresting death, a whole day nearer now,
Making all thought impossible but how
And where and when I shall myself die.

This acknowledgment of one's mortality looming out of the half-lit regions of sleeplessness would be cause enough for murdered sleep; the physical facts of sleeplessness themselves present unnatural and disturbing, even dangerous, causes for wakeful mental and physical anguish, as well. Dante Gabriel Rossetti, for example, suffered from a terrible, incurable insomnia that once drove him to a suicide attempt and forced his fatal addiction to chloral. And while an inherent loneliness and insomnia itself are reasons for disrupted sleep, there are others, also horrible and relentless: death, betrayal, terror, illness, loss of faith, lovelessness. Hopkins's nights were rent by unrequited prayer, Mirabai's by implacable, ecstatic longing for her absent "Dark One," Arthur Rimbaud's by drug-induced demons and guilt, Henry Wadsworth Longfellow's by unquenchable grieving for his dead wife, Shakespeare's Macbeth's by the horror of his inexorable black deeds. The speaker in Robert Hayden's "The Broken Dark" lies awake in his hospital bed, contemplating the very real possibility of his own obliteration. The condemned prisoner in Federico García Lorca's "Ballad of One Doomed to Die" knows that to close his eyes, even in sleep, is to surrender to his inevitable approaching fate.

Currents of loss and longing—John Keats's "wakeful anguish of the soul"—disturb the poems in this section. Insomnia seems at the very heart of the Petrarchan gestalt, and many of the Petrarchan poets and their ancestors and heirs—Sappho, Louise Labé, Sir Philip Sidney—found themselves up late, grieving for loves lost or unrequited. A fascinating "double-insomnia" charges several of these poems—in Sonnet 61, for example, Shakespeare's speaker imagines his love lying awake for happier reasons even as he wakefully and jealously frets: "For thee watch I whilst thou dost wake elsewhere/From me far off, with others all too near." In Meleagros' lyric, the speaker pushes his way inside his lover's dream, imagining her infidelity, and admonishes her lamp to wake her, to forbid such subconscious dalliances; Muriel Rukeyser is similarly aggressive in "Nevertheless the moon," invoking the moon's brilliant light to awaken and torture her lost love, even as she lies in anguish, remembering him. Job, "full of tossings to and fro unto the dawning of the day," feels that God Himself keeps an unrelenting and inexplicable vigil over his suffering: "Am I a sea, or a whale, that thou settest a watch over me?" he cries.

Whether abandoned by God or by love—whether robbed by death or by the fickleness of the human heart—the insomniac who wakes and feels Hopkins's "fell of dark, not day" is, again, deprived of more than sleep as he or she stares down the night. In the bereavement of a sleepless night, life itself can seem, as Hayden fears, a "shadow of deformed homunculus?/A fool's errand given by fools." And what, these poems ask, can be the outcome of even one such miserable night? Hopkins's desperate sense of his "sweating [self]; but worse"? Rimbaud's damnation? The irrefutable approach of Death, Larkin's sense of "what we know,/Have always known, know that we can't escape,/Yet can't accept"? Or Mark Strand's "lonely and . . . feckless end?"

Epiphany and Vision

Another source of the poetry of sleeplessness arises from a sense that the waking vision of sleep deprivation—even for one night—can remove the veils between sleep and waking, dream and reality, and invite spiritual, artistic, and erotic enlightenment, even redemption. Interestingly, while some sleep studies have suggested that chronic insomnia can cause severe disorientation and hallucination, others allege that a heightened sense of alertness, energy, and giddiness—a kind of "high"—can result from enforced wakefulness. Some therapists have even prescribed controlled insomnia as an antidepressant, and an old Dutch remedy for black moods is a nightlong dose of wakefulness. Perhaps this notion of an energizing, creative insomnia helps to account for the fact that a significant number of our greatest writers and thinkers were also chronic insomniacs. Thomas Alva Edison, for example, was, in the words of Nabokov, "a poor go-to-sleeper"—and it seems only fitting that one of Edison's most important inventions, the electric light bulb, has illuminated the insomnia of so many others over the years. Darwin was an insomniac. Franz Kafka felt that his insomnia was crucial to his work as a writer, finding in it not hopelessness but an opportunity to plunder the fecund, twilight realms between dream and waking. "I believe this sleeplessness comes only because I write," he wrote in his diary. And then, later, "If I can't pursue the stories through the nights, they break away and disappear."

We have only to examine the injunctions of Buddhist monks and other mystics and monastic orders against sleep, and their advocation of wakefulness and awareness at all times, to begin to appreciate the role of enforced wakefulness in reaching a kind of heightened spiritual awareness. The word *Buddha* originates in Sanskrit as "awakened," and the *Dhammapada* is replete with the repeated conviction that "Among the sleepers, the wide-awake,/The one with great wisdom moves on,/As a racehorse who leaves behind a nag." Hermits and monks, like the poet Ryōkan, harboring mosquitoes inside their kimono sleeves or soundly whacking each other in order to keep awake, found in the darkness around them Zen epiphanies of sound. In his *Meditations*, Marcus Aurelius, too, encouraged wakefulness: "When it is hard to shake off sleep, remind yourself that to be going about the duties you owe society is to be obeying the laws of man's nature and your own constitution, whereas sleep is something we share with the unreasoning brute creation," suggesting, perhaps, that insomnia itself might be even more natural—certainly more civilized—than slumber. The Bible is full of admonishments against sleep and of assurances that God is ever watchful, ever wakeful on our behalf ("he that keepeth Israel shall neither slumber nor sleep," in Psalm 121). This sense of God's insomnia is reinforced in John Milton's *Paradise Lost*, in which God, with his "unsleeping eyes," is portrayed as a kind of all-night, one-man watchtower, orchestrating a corps of vigilant angels on a course of eternal protection from a similarly wakeful Satan. The Inuit hunter in "Utitia'q's Song" spends a week adrift, lost on the ice, but finds that the enforced hardship of his wakefulness becomes a kind of transcendence: "When I tire of being awake/I begin to wake./It gives me joy." Umberto Saba speaks to the paradox of spiritual sleep deprivation when he diagnoses himself as "sick with insomnia,/a religious pleasure."

Other poems give us yet another occasion for fulfilled wakefulness, elated as their speakers are by the insomnia of the happier lover, awake in bed all night because of sexual and spiritual anticipation and fulfillment rather than Petrarchan yearning. The mystic Lalla, for example, expresses a nocturnal communion with God that is charged with erotic overtones, and John Berryman's sleeplessness is suffused with the palpable music of reciprocal passion. Even Rossetti managed to turn his affliction of sleeplessness into a source of waking vision, where the veils separating dream and reality grow thin and, in "Insomnia," his speaker is granted an ecstatic glimpse of a distant love.

Poets like Emily Brontë saw visions at night and hungrily invoked sleeplessness as a wellspring of imagination, of poetry, and of salvation itself. Brontë felt most imaginatively alive at night, so much so that she craves, in "Stars," the inverted world of night, begging its celestial lights to "Let me sleep through [the sun's] blinding reign,/And only wake with you!" In "Bright Star," Keats invokes an ever-wakeful star, but not because he wishes merely to keep watch "with eternal lids apart," but because he'd like to be able, like the star's light, to fall upon his

. . . love's ripening breast,
To feel forever its soft fall and swell,
Awake forever in a sweet unrest . . .

For other poets, the connections between sleeplessness and art, insomnia and poetry, are even more overt and critical. "There are invisible bridges between sleep and waking," Octavio Paz has written, and they are crucial to poetry. Yannis Ritsos's "His Lamp Near Daybreak" is about the poet Constantine Cavafy writing a poem all night, and the resulting poems, both Ritsos's and Cavafy's, create "a glass bridge . . . /. . . joining,/now of his own free will, the night and the day." Such poets want, as Bernard Spencer writes, to "sweat the night into words," with sleeplessness often a metaphor or embodiment of the poem itself. Wallace Stevens's Berserk ("sharp he was/As the sleepless!"), for example, is a personification of the restless, primal imagination of the poet. In a very concrete and mimetic example of creative insomnia, Stéphane Mallarmé once spent a sleepless night of joy, expectation—and jealousy?—composing "Gift of the Poem" while his wife gave birth to a flesh-and-blood child. However vicarious or harsh the vision may be that results from the experience of insomnia—however "small-time" its paradise, as Charles Wright puts it—the salvaging of wakeful hours, the forging of what's "seen" at such a time into a poem, can be, for some, a kind of redemption. It's clear that for many poets/insomniacs, the connections between wakefulness and the impulses, reasons and passions out of which they write are undeniable, and powerfully resonant.

André Hodeir once said that Charlie Parker located melody in his soloing by playing all around it, embellishing, implying, and defining it by its absence. The insomniac flirts in such a way with "the other," with Night, with absence, with sleep—and with sleep's kissing cousins, unconsciousness and Death. When we sleep—our small, nocturnal death— the world disappears; when we're experiencing insomnia, the world also, in a sense, disappears—*it* falls asleep—and we are awake to *witness* it, which can be both frightening and exhilarating. A special vision emerges from the boons and banes of sleeplessness, and poems forged from night's isolation cast all human endeavor and questions in a more acute light. Poets remind us that insomnia, in all its insufferable and fruitful manifestations, is an experience shared across temporal and cultural boundaries; it can make us more aware of our own sleeping places, our own lit windows, our own watching and the dark we watch against. And who better to speak of this complicated experience than the poets among us? In the poem

"My night awake," Muriel Rukeyser considers "the poet/yet
unborn in this dark/who will be the throat of these
hours." Who, she asks, "will speak these days,/if not I,/if
not you?"

The Congress of the Insomniacs

CHARLES SIMIC

Mother of God, everyone is invited:
Stargazing Peruvian shepherds,
Old men on sidewalks of New York.
You, too, doll with eyes open
Listening to the rain next to a sleeping child.

A big hotel ballroom with mirrors on every side.
Think about it as you lie in the dark.
Angels on its ornate ceilings,
Naked nymphs in what must be paradise.

There's a stage, a lectern,
An usher with a flashlight.
Someone will address this gathering yet
From his bed of nails.
Sleeplessness is like metaphysics.
Be there.

. . . to be up late is to be up late . . .

—*Sir Andrew Aguecheek*
(*from Shakespeare's* Twelfth Night)

And out there,
in sight of some ultimate bakery
the street-light
of my insomnia.

—*Charles Simic*
(*from* "Euclid Avenue")

· PART ONE ·

SOLITUDE
& VIGIL

ELIZABETH BISHOP

The moon in the bureau mirror
looks out a million miles
(and perhaps with pride, at herself,
but she never, never smiles)
far and away beyond sleep, or
perhaps she's a daytime sleeper.

By the Universe deserted,
she'd tell it to go to hell,
and she'd find a body of water,
or a mirror, on which to dwell.
So wrap up care in a cobweb
and drop it down the well

into that world inverted
where left is always right,
where the shadows are really the body,
where we stay awake all night,
where the heavens are shallow as the sea
is now deep, and you love me.

Insomnia

JOYCE CAROL OATES

Lie down in sleep but suddenly
this windowless bathroom?
white-glaring tiles? porcelain
sink so fiercely scoured
it's dancing with flames?
and no shadowy corners?
and the chrome faucets
too hot to touch? and
the perfect pool of the toilet
bowl in which a single eyeball
floats? and the mirror
so polished there's nothing
beyond the surface not even
                    you?

ALEXANDER PUSHKIN

I can't sleep; no light burns;
All round, darkness, irksome sleep.
Only the monotonous
Ticking of the clock,
The old wives' chatter of fate,
Trembling of the sleeping night,
Mouse-like scurrying of life . . .
Why do you disturb me?
What do you mean, tedious whispers?
Is it the day I have wasted
Reproaching me or murmuring?
What do you want from me?
Are you calling me or prophesying?
I want to understand you,
I seek a meaning in you . . .

—*Translated from the Russian by D. M. Thomas*

Insomnia

DANA GIOIA

Now you hear what the house has to say.
Pipes clanking, water running in the dark,
the mortgaged walls shifting in discomfort,
and voices mounting in an endless drone
of small complaints like the sounds of a family
that year by year you've learned how to ignore.

But now you must listen to the things you own,
all that you've worked for these past years,
the murmur of property, of things in disrepair,
the moving parts about to come undone,
and twisting in the sheets remember all
the faces you could not bring yourself to love.

How many voices have escaped you until now,
the venting furnace, the floorboards underfoot,
the steady accusations of the clock
numbering the minutes no one will mark.
The terrible clarity this moment brings,
the useless insight, the unbroken dark.

CORNELIUS EADY

You'll never sleep tonight.
Trains will betray you, cars confess
Their destinations,

Whether you like it
Or not.

They want more
Than to be in
Your dreams.

They want to tell you
A story.

They yammer all night and then
The birds take over,
Jeering as only
The well-rested can.

Mirrors at 4 A.M.

CHARLES SIMIC

You must come to them sideways
In rooms webbed in shadow,
Sneak a view of their emptiness
Without them catching
A glimpse of you in return.

The secret is,
Even the empty bed is a burden to them,
A pretense.
They are more themselves keeping
The company of a blank wall,
The company of time and eternity

Which, begging your pardon,
Cast no image
As they admire themselves in the mirror,
While you stand to the side
Pulling a hanky out
To wipe your brow surreptitiously.

PATUMAṈĀR

The still drone of the time
past midnight.
All words put out,
men are sunk into the sweetness
of sleep. Even the far-flung world
has put aside its rages
for sleep.

       Only I
am awake.

—*Translated from the Tamil by A. K. Ramanujan*

The Moon

GUNNAR EKELÖF

The moon passes her hands softly over my eyes,
wakes me long into the night. Lonesome
    among the sleepers,
I lay wood on the fire, fuss about with smoking
    sticks,
move quietly among the shadows, shadows
    flapping high
on the brown logs, richly
decorated with glistening fish-lures . . .

Why did you wake me? Lonesome among the
    sleepers,
backs turned to the fire, I open the door quietly,
walk around the corner in the snow, tramp in
    my fur boots,
moonshine coldly calling me over the snow . . .

—*Translated from the Swedish by Robert Bly*

WALT WHITMAN

I wander all night in my vision,
Stepping with light feet, swiftly and noiselessly
    stepping and stopping,
Bending with open eyes over the shut eyes of
    sleepers,
Wandering and confused, lost to myself, ill-
    assorted, contradictory,
Pausing, gazing, bending, and stopping.

How solemn they look there, stretch'd and still,
How quiet they breathe, the little children in
    their cradles.

The wretched features of ennuyés, the white
    features of corpses, the livid faces of
    drunkards, the sick-gray faces of onanists,
The gash'd bodies on battle-fields, the insane in
    their strong-door'd rooms, the sacred idiots,
    the new-born emerging from gates, and the
    dying emerging from gates,
The night pervades them and infolds them.

The married couple sleep calmly in their bed,
  he with his palm on the hip of the wife, and
  she with her palm on the hip of her husband,
The sisters sleep lovingly side by side in their bed,
The men sleep lovingly side by side in theirs,
And the mother sleeps with her little child
  carefully wrapt.

The blind sleep, and deaf and dumb sleep,
The prisoner sleeps well in the prison, the
  runaway son sleeps,
The murderer that is to be hung next day, how
  does he sleep?
And the murder'd person, how does he sleep?

The female that loves unrequited sleeps,
And the male that loves unrequited sleeps,
The head of the money-maker that plotted all
  day sleeps,
And the enraged and treacherous dispositions,
  all, all sleep.

I stand in the dark with drooping eyes by the
    worst-suffering and the most restless,
I pass my hands soothingly to and fro a few
    inches from them,
The restless sink in their beds, they fitfully sleep.

Now I pierce the darkness, new beings appear,
The earth recedes from me into the night,
I saw that it was beautiful, and I see that what
    is not the earth is beautiful.

I go from bedside to bedside, I sleep close with
    the other sleepers each in turn,
I dream in my dream all the dreams of the
    other dreamers,
And I become the other dreamers.

Acquainted with the Night

ROBERT FROST

I have been one acquainted with the night.
I have walked out in rain—and back in rain.
I have outwalked the furthest city light.

I have looked down the saddest city lane.
I have passed by the watchman on his beat
And dropped my eyes, unwilling to explain.

I have stood still and stopped the sound of feet
When far away an interrupted cry
Came over houses from another street,

But not to call me back or say good-by;
And further still at an unearthly height
One luminary clock against the sky

Proclaimed the time was neither wrong nor right.
I have been one acquainted with the night.

WILLIAM SHAKESPEARE

KING

How many thousand of my poorest subjects
Are at this hour asleep! O sleep, O gentle sleep,
Nature's soft nurse, how have I frighted thee,
That thou no more wilt weigh my eyelids down
And steep my senses in forgetfulness?
Why rather, sleep, liest thou in smoky cribs,
Upon uneasy pallets stretching thee,
And hushed with buzzing night-flies to thy
    slumber,
Than in the perfumed chambers of the great,
Under the canopies of costly state,
And lulled with sound of sweetest melody?
O thou dull god, why liest thou with the vile
In loathsome beds, and leavest the kingly couch
A watch-case or a common 'larum-bell?
Wilt thou upon the high and giddy mast
Seal up the ship-boy's eyes, and rock his brains
In cradle of the rude imperious surge
And in the visitation of the winds,
Who take the ruffian billows by the top,

Curling their monstrous heads and hanging them
With deafening clamor in the slippery clouds,
That, with the hurly, death itself awakes?
Canst thou, O partial sleep, give thy repose
To the wet sea-son in an hour so rude,
And, in the calmest and most stillest night,
With all appliances and means to boot,
Deny it to a king? Then happy low, lie down!
Uneasy lies the head that wears a crown.

OSIP MANDELSTAM

Insomnia. Homer. Taut sails.
I've read to the middle of the list of ships:
the strung-out flock, the stream of cranes
that once rose above Hellas.

Flight of cranes crossing strange borders,
leaders drenched with the foam of the gods,
where are you sailing? What would Troy be
    to you,
men of Achaea, without Helen?

The sea—Homer—it's all moved by love. But
    to whom
shall I listen? No sound now from Homer,
and the black sea roars like a speech
and thunders up the bed.

—*Translated from the Russian by Clarence Brown and W. S. Merwin*

Insomnia Song
GREGORY ORR

Is it me tossing
or is this bed
a small boat
in an unprotected
cove?
    Haul
anchor, I suppose.
That is: turn on
a light and read
all night.
    Book
open on my knees;
its pages: white
sails spread.

Fleeing hell,
that's in the head.

HERMAN MELVILLE

In bed I muse on Tenier's boors,
Embrowned and beery losels all:
    A wakeful brain
    Elaborates pain:
Within low doors the slugs of boors
Laze and yawn and doze again.

In dreams they doze, the drowsy boors,
Their hazy hovel warm and small:
    Thought's ampler bound
    But chill is found:
Within low doors the basking boors
Snugly hug the ember-mound.

Sleepless, I see the slumberous boors
Their blurred eyes blink, their eyelids fall:
    Thought's eager sight
    Aches—overbright!
Within low doors the boozy boors
Cat-naps take in pipe-bowl light.

Sleep's Underside

MELISSA KIRSCH

Blaze awake in the night and detest
the gamelan, the car horns insist that
you do: they clamor on, imitate
the gongs, their timbres rowdy and dissonant.
The night-clangs, the galumphing
passersby, the mosquito's crescendoing trill
all conspire: they want you up,
reassimilating. They want you
supine on the rag rug watching
the light lighten from black
to grey. They want
you to absorb it in porefuls.

Insomnia is dull now, even
common. What you have is
too much time. Enough to visualize
day, which is sad and false
as carnivals are, all pinwheels
and peanut brittle and beholden
to the idea of brightness
as paradise. In this spectacle,

you'll lug your own tired body,

its heft of bone and muscle
sagging uncompliantly,
invoking the ground.

Insomnia

DEBRA NYSTROM

It's the ceaseless wind
off the prairie, blasting
grit into the window casings,
snapping one brittle weed against
the pane, rousing rattlesnakes—
blinded in this season
of shedding skins, they will strike
at any vibration.

Try to lie without moving,
think nothing, sink,
follow the exposed poplar roots
that crowd to the lip
of the cistern's cool, cement lid:
within, broader than
a man's arm-span, three times deeper
than his height, the wet dark
of the slick-sided cylinder
does not admit wind
or snake. But I am too weak
to lift the lid alone.

CAO BÁ QUÁT

The self must hide from wind and dust—
the door is always tightly shut.
I strive to nurse a simple soul,
open to images of yore.
A still, hushed place fit for Tzu-yün:
a bed all lined with books and books.
I toss and turn with my own thoughts,
half in a drowse and half awake.
I wish for blessings, hum "Sang-hu."
I long for wisdom, chant "Hsi-ling."
Who has preserved those age-old norms
to act as my exemplar now?
At sunset creatures take their rest.
High heavens hold a deep, deep night.
Below, there lies a sleepless man.
Above, a star's about to fall.
Cocks on their perches seem to dance.
Lone orchids in the dark smell sweet.
I'll sing and lift my voice through space—
but its faint echo who will hear?

—*Translated from the Vietnamese by Huỳnh Sanh Thông*
 (Originally written in Chinese)

The Insomnia of Tremayne
DONALD JUSTICE

The all-night stations—Tremayne pictures them
As towers that shoot great sparks off through
        the dark—
Fade out and drift among the drifted hours
Just now returning to his bedside clock;
And something starts all over, call it day.
He likes, he really likes the little hum,
Which is the last sound of all nightsounds
        to decay.

Call that the static of the spheres, a sound
Of pure inbetweenness, far, and choked, and thin.
As long as it lasts—a faint, celestial surf—
He feels no need to dial the weather in,
Or music, or the news, or anything.
And it soothes him, like some night-murmuring
        nurse,
Murmuring nothing much perhaps, but
        murmuring.

SALVATORE QUASIMODO

Necropolis of Pantàlica
A glad gust of winged things
jarring the green light:
the sea in the leaves.

I am awry. And all that's born in me to joy
time lacerates, leaving only
its faint echo in voice of trees.

My self-love—lost,
memory, not human:
on the dead, celestial stigmata glisten,
grave starshapes fall into the rivers:
An hour grows languid with soft rain
or a song stirs in this eternal night.

Years and years, I sleep
in an open cell of my earth,
seaweed shoulders against gray waters:
in the still air meteors thunder.

—*Translated from the Italian by Allen Mandelbaum*

Halcion

R.T. SMITH

for Hayden Carruth

Having allowed my willow to dry out
while I traveled in August dust
and rumors of drought back home,
I found it dreary, brown, the leaves
all dropped or trussed up by bagworms
when I returned, so for once it was
lucky—my insomnia, I mean—as I
devised a routine of downing
my blue Halcion tablet at midnight
and watering the lawn where pine
needles and sphagnum moss surround
the trunk as big around as my arm,
but as I said, dying. I had about
an hour before drowsing, and it was
hard not to watch the stars
and consider the name of my wonder
drug while seeking the Pleiades
where Alcyone was said to have gone
after myth closed off for science.
I have always loved the notion

of her and the drowned Ceyx
after some god took pity on her
grief and changed them both
to kingfishers, calming the winds
to what we call *halcyon days*,
after the bird's name in Greek,
and God knows I was calm those nights,
my blood spelled by medication,
till I heard the radio reports
in October that the stuff had side
effects—depression and persecution
dreams—so I dropped that regimen,
went back to turgid books in bed
and a glass of wine, the supple limbs
having greened forth newly anyway,
the loblolly and twin honey locust
doing fine all along without any
supplemental attention, but none
of that absolving me of responsibility
to make provisions if I wish
to pilgrim abroad and still celebrate
on the edge of sleep the fountaining-
out of *Salix babylonica*, my one
thirsty willow and comfort-of-home.

Insomniac

SYLVIA PLATH

The night sky is only a sort of carbon paper,
Blueblack, with the much-poked periods of stars
Letting in the light, peephole after peephole—
A bonewhite light, like death, behind all things.
Under the eyes of the stars and the moon's rictus
He suffers his desert pillow, sleeplessness
Stretching its fine, irritating sand in all directions.

Over and over the old, granular movie
Exposes embarrassments—the mizzling days
Of childhood and adolescence, sticky with dreams,
Parental faces on tall stalks, alternately stern
        and tearful,
A garden of buggy roses that made him cry.
His forehead is bumpy as a sack of rocks.
Memories jostle each other for face-room like
        obsolete film stars.

He is immune to pills: red, purple, blue—
How they lit the tedium of the protracted
    evening!
Those sugary planets whose influence won
    for him
A life baptized in no-life for a while,
And the sweet, drugged waking of a
    forgetful baby.
Now the pills are worn-out and silly, like
    classical gods.
Their poppy-sleepy colors do him no good.

His head is a little interior of gray mirrors.
Each gesture flees immediately down an alley
Of diminishing perspectives, and its significance
Drains like water out the hole at the far end.
He lives without privacy in a lidless room,
The bald slots of his eyes stiffened wide-open
On the incessant heat-lightning flicker
    of situations.

48   Nightlong, in the granite yard, invisible cats
      Have been howling like women, or damaged
            instruments.
      Already he can feel daylight, his white disease,
      Creeping up with her hatful of trivial repetitions.
      The city is a map of cheerful twitters now,
      And everywhere people, eyes mica-silver
            and blank,
      Are riding to work in rows, as if recently
            brainwashed.

LOUISE GLÜCK

A lady weeps at a dark window.
Must we say what it is? Can't we simply say
a personal matter? It's early summer;
next door the Lights are practising
    klezmer music.
A good night: the clarinet is in tune.

As for the lady—she's going to wait forever;
there's no point in watching longer.
After awhile, the streetlight goes out.

But is waiting forever
always the answer? Nothing
is always the answer; the answer
depends on the story.

Such a mistake to want
clarity above all things. What's
a single night, especially
one like this, now so close to ending?
On the other side, there could be anything,
all the joy in the world, the stars fading,
the streetlight becoming a bus stop.

Insomnia at the Solstice

JANE KENYON

The quicksilver song
of the wood thrush spills
downhill from ancient maples
at the end of the sun's single most
altruistic day. The woods grow dusky
while the bird's song brightens.

Reading to get sleepy . . . Rabbit
Angstrom knows himself so well,
why isn't he a better man?
I turn out the light, and rejoice
in the sound of high summer, and in air
on bare shoulders—*dolce, dolce*—
no blanket, or even a sheet.
A faint glow remains over the lake.

Now come wordless contemplations
on love and death, worry about
money, and the resolve to have the vet
clean the dog's teeth, though
he'll have to anaesthetize him.

An easy rain begins, drips off
the edge of the roof, onto the tin
watering can. A vast irritation rises . . . .
I turn and turn, try one pillow,
two, think of people who have no beds.

A car hisses by on wet macadam.
Then another. The room turns
gray by insensible degrees. The thrush
begins again its outpouring of silver
to rich and poor alike, to the just
and the unjust.

The dog's wet nose appears
on the pillow, pressing lightly,
decorously. He needs to go out.
All right cleverhead, let's declare
a new day.
        Washing up, I say
to the face in the mirror,
"You're still here! How you bored me
all night, and now I'll have
to entertain you all day . . . ."

When Night is almost done

EMILY DICKINSON

When Night is almost done—
And Sunrise grows so near
That we can touch the Spaces—
It's time to smooth the Hair—

And get the Dimples ready—
And wonder we could care
For that old—faded Midnight—
That frightened—but an Hour—

WELDON KEES

If this room is our world, then let
This world be damned. Open this roof
For one last monstrous flood
To sweep away this floor, these chairs,
This bed that takes me to no sleep.
Under the black sky of our circumstance,
Mumbling of wet barometers, I stare
At citied dust that soils the glass
While thunder perishes. The heroes perish
Miles from here. Their blood runs heavy in
    the grass,
Sweet, restless, clotted, sickening,
Runs to the rivers and the seas, the seas
That are the source of that devouring flood
That I await, that I must perish by.

Midnight Saving Time
ADRIEN STOUTENBURG

How to deal with these hours,
alone under the ceiling's black canopy
while the clock multiplies its two fingers
into ten, eleven, twelve,
cracks its knuckles at midnight,
builds an exclamation point,
then starts all over again?

My pillow smells of smoke,
skin lotions, gin, and something wilder,
almost out of time,
as when some other anxious head, on rock
or weeds, rolled in a vision
of a world being born
out of an animal stink and splen-
dor;
invented an upright spine
and walked this way
and to this room
to stand in his primordial hair,

hand grasping mine.
    Cousin, your cave was better than you knew.
    Except for you, we might have stayed
    beyond the mind's chill blast,
    the wheel's hot, greasy stride,
    scratching our fleas
    but wrapped in snores
beside a warm, exhausted mate,
our only clock a waterfall or gonging moon.

I await, awake, the gadgetries of day—
the percolator plugged into my veins,
the toaster clicking with my borrowed nerves,
and then the traffic's grinding games,
my blood a pawn, all hours blown
down office shafts and streets and bars
until, again, the pitch and pall of night.

You with your shaggy eye and reach
would have saved at least some bone from these.
I munch on air, not knowing how to use
either my darkness or my light.

LOUISE BOGAN

It was a waning crescent
Dark on the wrong side
On which one does not wish
Setting in the hour before daylight
For my sleepless eyes to look at.

O, as a symbol of dis-hope
Over the July fields,
Dissolving, waning.
In spite of its sickle shape.

I saw it and thought it new
In that short moment
That makes all symbols lucky
Before we read them rightly.

Down to the dark it swam,
Down to the dark it moved,
Swift to that cluster of evenings
When curved toward the full it sharpens.

MARK JARMAN

The new day cancels dread
 And dawn forgives all sins,
All the judgments of insomnia,
 As if they were only dreams.

The ugly confrontation
 After midnight, with the mirror,
Turns white around the edges
 And burns away like frost.

Daylight undoes gravity
 And lightness responds to the light.
The new day lifts all weight,
 Like stepping off into space.

Where is that room you woke to,
 By clock-light, at 3 a.m.?
Nightmare's many mansions,
 Falling, have taken it with them.

58 The new day, the day's newness,
      And the wretchedness that, you thought,
      Would never, never depart,
        Meet—and there is goodbye.

    A bad night lies ahead
      And a new day beyond that—
    A simple sequence, but hard
      To remember in the right order.

And finally there was the sleepless night
When I decided to explore and fight
The foul, the inadmissible abyss,
Devoting all my twisted life to this
One task.

—Vladimir Nabokov (*from Pale Fire*)

· PART TWO ·

ANGUISH &
LONGING

If only sleep would come, as it has come
on other nights, already slipping through
my thoughts.
        Instead now
like an old washerwoman wringing clothes,
anguish wrings another pain from my heart.
I would cry out, but cannot. As for torment—
suffered once—I suffer on in silence.

Ah, that which I have lost, only I know.

Translated from the Italian by Felix Stefanile

I wake and feel the fell of dark, not day

GERARD MANLEY HOPKINS

I wake and feel the fell of dark, not day.
What hours, O what black hours we have spent
This night! what sights you, heart, saw, ways
    you went!
And more must, in yet longer light's delay.
With witness I speak this. But where I say
Hours I mean years, mean life. And my lament
Is cries countless, cries like dead letters sent
To dearest him that lives alas! away.
I am gall, I am heartburn. God's most
    deep decree
Bitter would have me taste: my taste was me;
Bones built in me, flesh filled, blood brimmed
    the curse.
Selfyeast of spirit a dull dough sours. I see
The lost are like this, and their scourge to be
As I am mine, their sweating selves; but worse.

YUSEF KOMUNYAKAA

Laughing, with a TV's blue-static figures
   dancing through the air at 2 A.M.
with eight empty beer bottles lined up
   on the kitchen table, a full moon
gazing through the opened back door,
   his thick fingers drumming the pink
laminex, singing along with a rock video
   of soft porno, recounting dead friends,
with a tally of all his mistakes
   in front of him, after he's punched
the walls & refrigerator with his fist,
   unable to forget childhood's lonely
grass & nameless flowers & insects,
   crying for his black cat
hit by a car, drawing absent faces
   on the air with his right index finger,
rethinking lost years of a broken marriage
   like a wrecked ship inside a green bottle,
puffing a horn-shaped ceramic pipe,
   dragging his feet across the floor
in a dance with the shadow of a tree

on a yellow wall, going to the wooden fence
     to piss under the sky's marsupial stare,
        walking back in to pop the cap
   on his last beer, hugging himself awake,
        picking up a dried wishbone
   from the table & snapping it, cursing the world,
        softly whispering his daughter's name,
   he disturbs the void that is
        heavy as the heart's clumsy logbook.

ARTHUR RIMBAUD

Decidedly we are out of the world. No longer any sound. My sense of touch has left me. Ah! my castle, my Saxony, my willow wood. Evenings, mornings, nights, days . . . How weary I am!

I should have my hell for anger, my hell for pride,—and the hell of laziness; a symphony of hells.

I die of lassitude. It is the tomb, I go to the worms, horror of horrors! Satan, you fraud, you would dissolve me with your charms. I insist. I insist! a thrust of the pitchfork, a drop of fire.

Ah! to rise again into life! to cast our eyes on our deformities. And that poison, that kiss, a thousand times accursed! My weakness, the cruelty of the world! My God, pity, hide me, I behave too badly!—I am hidden and I am not.

It is the fire that flares up again with its damned.

Translated from the French by Louise Varèse

As a servant earnestly desireth the shadow, and as an hireling looketh for the reward of his work;

So am I made to possess months of vanity, and wearisome nights are appointed to me.

When I lie down, I say, When shall I arise, and the night be gone? and I am full of tossings to and fro unto the dawning of the day.

My flesh is clothed with worms and clods of dust; my skin is broken, and become loathsome.

My days are swifter than a weaver's shuttle, and are spent without hope.

O remember that my life is wind: mine eye shall no more see good.

The eye of him that hath seen me shall see me no more: thine eyes are upon me, and I am not.

Am I a sea, or a whale, that thou settest a watch over me?

When I say, My bed shall comfort me, my couch shall ease my complaint;

Then thou scarest me with dreams, and terrifiest me
through visions;

So that my soul chooseth strangling, and death rather
than my life.

I have sinned: what shall I do unto thee, O thou Preserv-
er of men? why hast thou set me as a mark against thee, so
that I am a burden to myself?

And why dost thou not pardon my transgression, and
take away mine iniquity? for now shall I sleep in the dust;
and thou shalt seek me in the morning, but I shall not be.

Lament at Night

H. LEIVICK

At midnight I would hear my father rise
And chant the threnody for Zion's fall.
I envy him his prayer—for fifty years
That cry pursues me, mourning over all.

And yet I do the things my father did;
I mourn for ruin and the guiltless dead;
Like him I bite my lip and grit my teeth,
But this I lack—his beard of flaming red.

In fifty years, I wonder, will my sons
Long after me with the same love and pain?
Will they start up at night trembling and awed,
Some line I wrote upon their lips again?

Should that be so—then hear me, Lord of Time,
And show this mercy to these sons of mine:
Erase, wipe clean, as chalk is wiped from slate
My nights, my dreadful nights, of nineteen
        thirty-nine.

Translated from the Yiddish by Marie Syrkin

Evening rises toward the mountain trails
as I climb up to my high chamber.

Thin clouds lodge along the cliffs.
A lonely moon rocks slowly on the waves.

A line of cranes flaps silently overhead,
and, far off, a howling pack of wolves.

Sleepless, memories of war betray me:
I am powerless against the world.

Translated from the Chinese by Sam Hamill

Ballad of One Doomed to Die

FEDERICO GARCÍA LORCA

Loneliness without rest!
The little eyes of my body
and the big eyes of my horse
never close at night
nor look that other way
where quietly disappears
a dream of thirteen boats.
Instead, clean and hard,
squires of wakefulness,
my eyes look for a north
of metals and of cliffs
where my veinless body
consults frozen playing cards.

Heavy water-oxen charge
boys who bathe in the moons
of their rippling horns.
And the hammers sing
on the somnambulous anvils
the insomnia of the rider
and the insomnia of the horse.

On the twenty-fifth of June
they said to Amargo:
—Now, you may cut, if you wish,
the oleanders in your courtyard.
Paint a cross on your door
and put your name beneath it,
for hemlock and nettle
shall take root in your side
and needles of wet lime
will bite into your shoes.
It will be night, in the dark,
in the magnetic mountains
where water-oxen drink
in the reeds, dreaming.
Ask for lights and bells.
Learn to cross your hands,
to taste the cold air
of metals and of cliffs
because within two months
you'll lie down shrouded.

Santiago moved his misty
sword in the air.
Dead silence flows over

the shoulder of the curved sky.
On the twenty-fifth of June
Amargo opened his eyes,
and the twenty-fifth of August
he lay down to close them.
Men came down the street
to look upon the doomed one
who cast on the wall his shadow
of loneliness at rest.
And the impeccable sheet
with its hard Roman accent
gave death a certain poise
by the rectitude of its folds.

Translated from the Spanish by Langston Hughes

ROBERT HAYDEN

Sleepless, I stare
from the dark hospital room
at shadows of a flower and its leaves
the nightlight fixes like a blotto
on the corridor wall. Shadow-plays
of Bali—demons move to the left,
gods, in their frangipani crowns
and gold, to the right.
Ah and my life
in the shadow of God's laser light—
shadow of deformed homunculus?
A fool's errand given by fools.
Son, go fetch a pint of pigeon's milk
from the drugstore and be quick.
Demons on the left. Death on either side,
the Rabbi said, the way of life between.
That groaning. Man with his belly slashed,
two-timing lover. Dying?
The nightnurse rustles by.
Struggles in the pit. I have come back

76   to tell thee of struggles in the pit.
Perhaps is dying.
Free of pain, my own death still
a theorem to be proved.
Alláh' u' Abhá. O Healing Spirit,
Thy nearness our forgiving cure.

WILLIAM SHAKESPEARE

MACBETH

There's one did laugh in 's sleep, and one
    cried 'Murder!'
That they did wake each other. I stood and
    heard them.
But they did say their prayers and address'd them
Again to sleep.

LADY MACBETH

There are two lodged together.

MACBETH

One cried 'God bless us' and 'Amen' the other,
As they had seen me with these hangman's hands.
Listening their fear, I could not say 'Amen,'
When they did say 'God bless us.'

LADY MACBETH

Consider it not so deeply.

MACBETH

But wherefore could not I pronounce 'Amen?'
I had most need of blessing, and 'Amen'
Stuck in my throat.

These deeds must not be thought
After these ways; so, it will make us mad.

MACBETH
Methought I heard a voice cry, 'Sleep no more!
Macbeth does murder sleep'—the innocent sleep,
Sleep that knits up the ravel'd sleave of care,
The death of each day's life, sore labor's bath,
Balm of hurt minds, great nature's
     second course,
Chief nourisher in life's feast,—

LADY MACBETH
What do you mean?

MACBETH
Still it cried 'Sleep no more' to all the house;
'Glamis hath murder'd sleep, and
     therefore Cawdor
Shall sleep no more: Macbeth shall sleep
     no more.'

Last night, I heard your mother,
my sister, crying in her sleep.
She was sleeping with my mother,
who is deaf, and did not wake
to comfort her. Mother and daughter
sleeping in one bed,
trying to make the world whole again.
My mother was there
to make losing you less
painful. But it is
painful. All day
they both had cried,
praying for strength.
I remember saying,
as though it would help,
as though it were true,
there is nothing we can do
to bring him back.
Now strength and rest will come
from what we suffer.
I even made a little metaphor,

stolen from the Bible:
the sun will rise from the darkness.
But last night, dreaming of you
lost in the river, your mother
kept crying,
your grandmother kept sleeping,
and I kept lying
there in the dark
as if I were you,
the dead child,
unable or unwilling to hear.
Andrew, I am sorry:
I always believed in words,
and sent them instead of my body
to comfort the ones I love,
your mother and grandmother,
my sister and mother,
and Andrew, I did not rise
to put my arms around them.

HENRY WADSWORTH LONGFELLOW

In the long, sleepless watches of the night,
A gentle face—the face of one long dead—
Looks at me from the wall, where round
    its head
The night-lamp casts a halo of pale light.
Here in this room she died; and soul more white
Never through martyrdom of fire was led
To its repose; nor can in books be read
The legend of a life more benedight.
There is a mountain in the distant West
That, sun-defying, in its deep ravines
Displays a cross of snow upon its side.
Such is the cross I wear upon my breast
These eighteen years, through all the
    changing scenes
And seasons, changeless since the day she died.

Exile

ELLEN BRYANT VOIGT

The widow refuses sleep, for sleep pretends
that it can bring him back.
In this way,
the will is set against the appetite.
Even the empty hand moves to the mouth.
Apart from you,
I turn a corner in the city and find,
for a moment, the old climate,
the little blue flower everywhere.

Tonight I've watched

The moon and then
the Pleiades
go down

The night is now
half-gone; youth
goes; I am

in bed alone

Translated from the Greek by Mary Barnard

Aubade

PHILIP LARKIN

I work all day, and get half-drunk at night.
Waking at four to soundless dark, I stare.
In time the curtain-edges will grow light.
Till then I see what's really always there:
Unresting death, a whole day nearer now,
Making all thought impossible but how
And where and when I shall myself die.
Arid interrogation: yet the dread
Of dying, and being dead,
Flashes afresh to hold and horrify.

The mind blanks at the glare. Not in remorse
—The good not done, the love not given, time
Torn off unused—nor wretchedly because
An only life can take so long to climb
Clear of its wrong beginnings, and may never;
But at the total emptiness for ever,
The sure extinction that we travel to
And shall be lost in always. Not to be here,
Not to be anywhere,
And soon; nothing more terrible, nothing
        more true.

This is a special way of being afraid
No trick dispels. Religion used to try,
That vast moth-eaten musical brocade
Created to pretend we never die,
And specious stuff that says *No rational being*
Can fear a thing it will not feel, not seeing
That this is what we fear—no sight, no sound,
No touch or taste or smell, nothing to think with,
Nothing to love or link with,
The anaesthetic from which none come round.

And so it stays just on the edge of vision,
A small unfocused blur, a standing chill
That slows each impulse down to indecision.
Most things may never happen: this one will,
And realisation of it rages out
In furnace-fear when we are caught without
People or drink. Courage is no good:
It means not scaring others. Being brave
Lets no one off the grave.
Death is no different whined at than withstood.
Slowly light strengthens, and the room
    takes shape.
It stands plain as a wardrobe, what we know,
Have always known, know that we can't escape,

86 Yet can't accept. One side will have to go.
   Meanwhile telephones crouch, getting ready
         to ring
   In locked-up offices, and all the uncaring
   Intricate rented world begins to rouse.
   The sky is white as clay, with no sun.
   Work has to be done.
   Postmen like doctors go from house to house.

RITA DOVE

Although it is night, I sit in the
        bathroom, waiting.
Sweat prickles behind my knees, the baby-breasts
    are alert.
Venetian blinds slice up the moon; the tiles
    quiver in pale strips.

Then they come, the three seal men with eyes
    as round
As dinner plates and eyelashes like
    sharpened tines.
They bring the scent of licorice. One sits in
    the washbowl,

One on the bathtub edge; one leans against
    the door.
"Can you feel it yet?" they whisper.
I don't know what to say, again. They chuckle,

88   Patting their sleek bodies with their hands.
      "Well, maybe next time." And they rise,
      Glittering like pools of ink under moonlight,

      And vanish. I clutch at the ragged holes
      They leave behind, here at the edge of darkness.
      Night rests like a ball of fur on my tongue.

Dark One,
how can I sleep?
Since you left my bed
the seconds drag past like epochs,
each moment
a new torrent of pain.
I am no wife,
no lover comes through the darkness—
lamps, houses, no comfort.
On my couch
the embroidered flowers
pierce me like thistles,
   I toss through the night.

Yet who would believe my story?
That a lover
bit my hand like a snake,
and the venom bursts through
   and I'm dying?

90 I hear
     the peacock's faraway gospel,
     the nightingale's love song,
     the cuckoo—
     thickness on thickness folds through the sky,
     clouds flash with rain.
     Dark One, is there no love
     in this world
     that such anguish continues?
     Mira waits for a single
        glance from your eye.

Translated from the Rajasthani by Andrew Shelling

LOUISE LABÉ

Bright Venus, who across the heavens stray,
I pray you be my listener and witness;
My voice, while still your star is shining high,
Will bitterly lament its loving sickness.

My waking eye will melt more readily
When you are there to see, more tears will shed
Seeing your watching eye, more easily
Sorrow to weeping brims and soaks my bed.

Now human souls are all in love with sleep,
In gentle resting, restoration seek.
Too long the sunlight, pitiless and strong;

And when my heart is brought almost
       to breaking,
Then I to bed, lonely and tired of waking,
Retire and cry my pain out all night long.

Translated from the French by Graham Dunstan Martin

The Pains of Sleep

SAMUEL TAYLOR COLERIDGE

Ere on my bed my limbs I lay,
It hath not been my use to pray
With moving lips or bended knees;
But silently, by slow degrees,
My spirit I to Love compose,
In humble trust mine eye-lids close,
With reverential resignation,
No wish conceived, no thought exprest,
Only a sense of supplication;
A sense o'er all my soul imprest
That I am weak, yet not unblest,
Since in me, round me, every where
Eternal Strength and Wisdom are.

But yester-night I prayed aloud
In anguish and in agony,
Up-starting from the fiendish crowd
Of shapes and thoughts that tortured me:
A lurid light, a trampling throng,
Sense of intolerable wrong,
And whom I scorned, those only strong!
Thirst of revenge, the powerless will

Still baffled, and yet burning still!
Desire with loathing strangely mixed
On wild or hateful objects fixed.
Fantastic passions! maddening brawl!
And shame and terror over all!
Deeds to be hid which were not hid,
Which all confused I could not know
Whether I suffered, or I did:
For all seemed guilt, remorse or woe,
My own or others still the same
Life-stifling fear, soul-stifling shame.

So two nights passed: the night's dismay
Saddened and stunned the coming day.
Sleep, the wide blessing, seemed to me
Distemper's worst calamity.
The third night, when my own loud scream
Had waked me from the fiendish dream,
O'ercome with sufferings strange and wild,
I wept as I had been a child;
And having thus by tears subdued
My anguish to a milder mood,
Such punishments, I said, were due
To natures deepliest stained with sin,—
For aye entempesting anew

94   The unfathomable hell within,
      The horror of their deeds to view,
      To know and loathe, yet wish and do!
      Such griefs with such men well agree,
      But wherefore, wherefore fall on me?
      To be beloved is all I need,
      And whom I love, I love indeed.

For whatever animals dwell on earth,
except the few that hate the sun,
the time to labor is while it is day;
but when the sky lights up its stars
some return home and some make a nest in
    the wood
to have rest at least until the dawn.

And I—from when the lovely dawn begins
to scatter the shadows from about the earth,
awakening the animals in every wood—
I never have any truce from sighs with the sun;
and then when I see the stars flaming
I go weeping and longing for the day.

When the evening drives away the bright day,
and our darkness makes elsewhere a dawn,
I gaze full of care at the cruel stars
that have made me out of sensitive earth;
and I curse the day on which I saw the sun,
for it makes me seem a man raised in the woods.

Translated from the Italian by Robert M. Durling

Come sleep, Oh sleep, the certain knot of peace
SIR PHILIP SIDNEY

Come sleep, Oh sleep, the certain knot of peace,
The baiting place of wit, the balm of woe,
The poor man's wealth, the prisoner's release,
Th' indifferent judge between the high and low;
With shield of proof shield me from out
    the prease
Of those fierce darts Despair at me doth throw;
Oh make in me those civil wars to cease;
I will good tribute pay, if thou do so.
Take thou of me smooth pillows, sweetest bed,
A chamber deaf to noise and blind to light,
A rosy garland and a weary head;
And if these things, as being thine by right,
Move not thy heavy grace, thou shalt in me,
Livelier than elsewhere, Stella's image see.

WILLIAM SHAKESPEARE

Is it thy will thy image should keep open
My heavy eyelids to the weary night?
Dost thou desire my slumbers should be broken
While shadows like to thee do mock my sight?
Is it thy spirit that thou send'st from thee
So far from home into my deeds to pry,
To find out shames and idle hours in me,
The scope and tenure of thy jealousy?
O no, thy love, though much, is not so great;
It is my love that keeps mine eye awake,
Mine own true love that doth my rest defeat
To play the watchman ever for thy sake.
 For thee watch I whilst thou dost
    wake elsewhere,
 From me far off, with others all too near.

The Night Alone

MELEAGROS

O Night, O sleepless tossing, longing
    for Hêliodôra!
Poor eyes hot with tears in the lingering white
  dawn!
Is she lonely too? Is she dreaming of how
    I kissed
 her,
And dreaming so, does she turn to kiss
    the dream
 of me?
        —or a new love? a newer toy?
Forbid it, lamp!
See it never!
Did I not set you to guard her?

Translated from the Greek by Dudley Fitts

We said there'd be a celebration . . .
There wasn't.
And so I dressed for no apparent
reason in the height of fashion.

I waited for you till dawn,
All night I waited.
In the carafe—stagnant wine,
on the tables—stale bread.

And when day came upon the land
—and I knew it would remain there—
I took the flowers from my hair
with a withered hand.

Translated from the Romanian by Andrea Deletant and Brenda Walker

She Speaks to Her Husband, Asleep

ROBERT SCHULTZ

"Moonlight pearls on my breast like solder.
Hotter and hotter, the needlepoint glows
As sewn beads burn their pattern in—
A snowflake pattern, my newest gown.
The frozen ground of these perfect sheets
Is a skillet to me. The whole house seethes
With difficult heat, inconvenient dreams,
Our children twisting like spreading flames.
You burrow into your willful sleep.
I whisper deep in the well of your ear:
'I'm alive, I'm alive! Are you dead to me?' "

MURIEL RUKEYSER

Nevertheless the moon
Heightens the secret
Sleep long withheld
Dry for a rain of dreams—
Flies straight above me
White, hot-hearted,
Among the streaming
Firmament armies.
A monk of flames
Stands shaking in my heart
Where sleep might lie.

Where you all night have lain.
And now hang dreaming,
Faded acute, fade full,
Calling your cloudy fame,
A keen high nightlong cry.
Rises my silent, turning
Heart. Heart where my love

Might lie, try toward my love
    Flying, let go all need,
    Brighten and burn—
    Rain down, raging for life
    Light my love's dream tonight.

WILLIAM SHAKESPEARE

Weary with toil, I haste me to my bed,
The dear repose for limbs with travel tired,
But then begins a journey in my head
To work my mind when body's work's expired;
For then my thoughts, from far where I abide,
Intend a zealous pilgrimage to thee,
And keep my drooping eyelids open wide,
Looking on darkness which the blind do see;
Save that my soul's imaginary sight
Presents thy shadow to my sightless view,
Which, like a jewel hung in ghastly night,
Makes black night beauteous and her old
    face new.
 Lo, thus, by day my limbs, by night my mind,
 For thee and for myself no quiet find.

How can I then return in happy plight

WILLIAM SHAKESPEARE

How can I then return in happy plight,
That am debarred the benefit of rest,
When day's oppression is not eased by night,
But day by night and night by day oppressed,
And each, though enemies to either's reign,
Do in consent shake hands to torture me,
The one by toil, the other to complain
How far I toil, still farther off from thee?
I tell the day, to please him, thou art bright
And dost him grace when clouds do blot
     the heaven;
So flatter I the swart-complexioned night,
When sparkling stars twire not, thou gild'st
     the even.
  But day doth daily draw my sorrows longer,
  And night doth nightly make grief's
       strength seem stronger.

MARK STRAND

A man walks towards town,
a slack breeze smelling of earth
and the raw green of trees blows at his back.

He drags the weight of his passion as if nothing
    were over,
as if the woman, now curled in bed beside
    her lover,
still cared for him.

She is awake and stares at scars of light
trapped in the panes of glass.
He stands under her window, calling her name;

he calls all night and it makes no difference.
It will happen again, he will come back wherever
    she is.
Again he will stand outside and imagine

her eyes opening in the dark
and see her rise to the window and peer down.

Again she will lie awake beside her lover

and hear the voice from somewhere in the dark.
Again the late hour, the moon and stars,
the wounds of night that heal without sound,

again the luminous wind of morning that
        comes before the sun.
And, finally, without warning or desire,
the lonely and the feckless end.

The people need poetry that will be
    their own secret
to keep them awake forever,
and bathe them in the bright-haired wave
of its breathing.

—*Osip Mandelstam (from no. 355)*

Make music out of night will change
    the night.

—*Muriel Rukeyser (from "Night Music")*

• PART THREE •

EPIPHANY
& VISION

CHARLES WRIGHT

Full moon illuminated large initial for letter *M*,
Appalachian Book of the Dead, 22
    February 1997—
La luna piove, the moon rains down its
    antibiotic light
Over the sad, septic world,
Hieroglyphs on the lawn, supplicant whispers
    for the other side,
I am pure, I am pure, I am pure . . .

The soul is in the body as light is in the air,
Plotinus thought.
        Well, I wouldn't know about that, but
La luna piove, and shines out in every direction—
Under it all, disorder, above,
A handful of stars on one side, a handful on
    the other.
Whatever afflictions we have, we have them
    for good.

Such Egyptology in the wind, such
　　　raw brushstrokes,
Moon losing a bit from its left side at
　　　two o'clock.
Still, light mind-of-Godish,
　　　　silent deeps where seasons don't exist.
Surely some splendor's set to come forth,
Some last equation solved, declued
　　　and reclarified.
South wind and a long shine, a small-time
　　　paradiso.

KING TRẦN THÁI-TÔNG

Wind-swung, pine-shaded gate and
    moonlit court—
cool, pristine landscape after your own heart.
There lies a joy that no one else suspects:
the mountain hermit feasts on it till dawn.

Translated from the Vietnamese by Huỳnh Sanh Thông
(Originally written in Chinese)

FROM *Winter*

RYŌKAN

LATE AT night, listening to the winter rain,
recalling my youth—
Was it only a dream? Was I really young once?

THE HOUR grows late, but the sound of hail
striking the bamboo
Keeps me from sleep.

LYING in my freezing hut, unable to sleep;
only the quiet roar
Of water pouring over a cliff.

LATE AT night, the snow
is piling higher and higher,
Muffling the sound of the waterfall.

MY HEART beats faster and faster
and I cannot sleep.
Tomorrow will be the first day of spring!

Translated from the Japanese by John Stevens

I am happy.
    This is good.
There is nothing but ice all around.
    That is good.
    I am happy.
    This is good.
For land we have slush.
    That is good.
    I am happy.
    This is good.
When I do not know enough
    It is good.
When I tire of being awake
    I begin to wake.
    It gives me joy.

Adapted by Brian Swann
from the translation from the Inuit by Franz Boas

At the end of a crazy-moon night
the love of God rose.
I said, "It's me, Lalla."

The Beloved woke. We became That,
and the lake is crystal-clear.

*Translated from the Kashmiri, Hindi, and Sanskrit
by Coleman Barks*

STEPHEN MARGULIES

I.

In pain, in poverty, at night
The would-be sleeper
Shyly charms his illnesses:

Tile by tile silence is built,

Molecule by molecule warmth,

Breath by mantra breath the palm
And calm breast
Of the beloved's remembered sanity—

All alone
In pain

2.

Coda: Eyes Closed, Watching All Night for Winter
The stars are falling like snow
The leaves are falling like stars
My tears are falling like leaves
May the calm snow be firm with stars

Make the Bed

STEPHEN CUSHMAN

Behold the wreckage
of night, one heck
of a mess: covers
disheveled by love,
raucous, gymnastic,
or cast off in vast
deserts of insomnia
where trepidations bomb
tranquillity to rubble.
However this hub
of marriage got mangled,
the whole shebang
needs remaking.
So do it. Shake
out sheets and remember
He wanted them
brought in for sailing
female and male
to assure renewal.
Two by two,

Noah's pattern.
Remember that
when smoothing the wrinkled
comforter and think:
Rebuild the ark
before the darkness.

Insomnia

DANTE GABRIEL ROSSETTI

Thin are the night-skirts left behind
By daybreak hours that onward creep,
And thin, alas! the shred of sleep
That wavers with the spirit's wind:
But in half-dreams that shift and roll
And still remember and forget,
My soul this hour has drawn your soul
    A little nearer yet.

Our lives, most dear, are never near,
Our thoughts are never far apart,
Though all that draws us heart to heart
Seems fainter now and now more clear.
To-night Love claims his full control,
And with desire and with regret
My soul this hour has drawn your soul
    A little nearer yet.

Is there a home where heavy earth
Melts to bright air that breathes no pain,
Where water leaves no thirst again
And springing fire is Love's new birth?
If faith long bound to one true goal
May there at length its hope beget,
My soul that hour shall draw your soul
        For ever nearer yet.

White Night

MARY OLIVER

All night
  I float
    in the shallow ponds
      while the moon wanders
burning,
  bone white,
    among the milky stems.
      Once
I saw her hand reach
  to touch the muskrat's
    small sleek head
      and it was lovely, oh,
I don't want to argue anymore
  about all the things
    I thought I could not
      live without! Soon
the muskrat
  will glide with another
    into their castle
      of weeds, morning

will rise from the east
   tangled and brazen,
     and before that
       difficult
and beautiful
   hurricane of light
     I want to flow out
       across the mother
of all waters,
   I want to lose myself
     on the black
       and silky currents,
yawning,
   gathering
     the tall lilies
       of sleep.

Stars

EMILY BRONTË

Ah! why, because the dazzling sun
Restored our Earth to joy,
Have you departed, every one,
And left a desert sky?

All through the night, your glorious eyes
Were gazing down in mine,
And with a full heart's thankful sighs,
I blessed that watch divine.

I was at peace, and drank your beams
As they were life to me;
And revelled in my changeful dreams,
Like petrel on the sea.

Thought followed thought, star followed star,
Through boundless regions, on;
While one sweet influence, near and far,
Thrilled through, and proved us one!

Why did the morning dawn to break
So great, so pure, a spell;

And scorch with fire, the tranquil cheek,
Where your cool radiance fell?

Blood-red, he rose, and, arrow-straight,
His fierce beams struck my brow;
The soul of nature, sprang, elate,
But *mine* sank sad and low!

My lids closed down, yet through their veil,
I saw him, blazing, still,
And steep in gold the misty dale,
And flash upon the hill.

I turned me to the pillow, then,
To call back night, and see
Your worlds of solemn light, again,
Throb with my heart, and me!

It would not do—the pillow glowed,
And glowed both roof and floor;
And birds sang loudly in the wood,
And fresh winds shook the door;

126   The curtains waved, the wakened flies
       Were murmuring round my room,
       Imprisoned there, till I should rise,
       And give them leave to roam.

       Oh, stars, and dreams, and gentle night;
       Oh, night and stars return!
       And hide me from the hostile light,
       That does not warm, but burn;

       That drains the blood of suffering men;
       Drinks tears, instead of dew;
       Let me sleep through his blinding reign,
       And only wake with you!

JOHN KEATS

Bright star, would I were steadfast as thou art—
Not in lone splendor hung aloft the night
And watching, with eternal lids apart,
Like nature's patient, sleepless Eremite,
The moving waters at their priestlike task
Of pure ablution round earth's human shores,
Or gazing on the new soft fallen mask
Of snow upon the mountains and the moors—
No—yet still steadfast, still unchangeable,
Pillowed upon my fair love's ripening breast,
To feel forever its soft fall and swell,
Awake forever in a sweet unrest,
Still, still to hear her tender-taken breath,
And so live ever—or else swoon to death.

Owl

ROBERT MEZEY

Nightlong waiting and listening, being schooled
To long lying awake without thoughts,
I hear him calling from the other world.
A long silence, and then two flutey notes—
The cry of nobody, but urgent, cool,
Full of foreboding. He's in the cedar tree
Not twenty feet beyond my window sill;
The other world is very far away.
When, towards morning, he ceases, the
    air seems
More visible, although it's not yet light,
The black sky drained and all our
    speechless dreams
Fading into thought. Lord of the night,
Thy kingdom in which everything is one,
Come, speak to me, speak to me once again.

UMBERTO SABA

I've positioned myself to relax
under the stars,
one of those nights
sick with insomnia,
a religious pleasure.
My pillow is a rock.

A few feet away sits a dog.
He sits immobile and guards
the same distant point.
He's thinking.
He's thinking he's part of a rite.
Through his body
silences pass from the infinite.

Under a sky this blue,
on a night as rich with stars,
Jacob dreamed a ladder of angels
scaling the sky from his pillow
which was a rock.
Beneath countless stars,

the young man counted
        his offspring to come;
        on the same spot where he'd fled Esau's anger
        his more powerful brother,
        he imagined an empire
        more powerful and crowned
        with his own children's riches.
        What made him jump from his dream
        was the God that fought with him.

        Translated from the Italian by Christopher Millis

Insomnia, impalpable Creature!
Is all your love in your head
That you come and are ravished to see
Beneath your evil eye man gnaw
His sheets and twist himself with spleen,
Beneath your black diamond eye?

Tell me: why, during the sleepless night,
Rainy like a Sunday,
Do you come to lick us like a dog?
Hope or Regret that keeps watch,
Why, in our throbbing ear
Do you speak low . . . and say nothing?

Why to our parched throat
Do you always tilt your empty cup
And leave us stretching our neck,
Tantaluses, thirsters for chimeras—
Amorous philter or bitter dregs,
Cool dew or melted lead!
Insomnia, aren't you beautiful? . . .

Well, why, lascivious virgin,
Do you squeeze us between your knees?
Why do you moan on our lips,
Why do you unmake our bed,
And . . . not go to bed with us?

Why, impure night-blooming beauty,
That black mask on your face? . . .
To fill the golden dreams with intrigue? . . .
Aren't you love in space,
The breath of Messaline weary
But still not satisfied?

Insomnia, are you Hysteria? . . .
Are you the barrel organ
Which grinds out the hosanna of the elect? . . .
Or aren't you the eternal plectrum
On the nerves of the damned-of-letters
Scraping out their verses—which only they
have read?

Insomnia, are you the troubled donkey
Of Buridan—or the firefly
Of hell? —Your kiss of fire
Leaves a chilled taste of red-hot iron . . .
Oh, come perch in my hovel! . . .
We will sleep together a while.

Translated from the French by Kenneth Koch and Georges Guy

A Clear Midnight
WALT WHITMAN

This is thy hour O Soul, thy free flight into the
wordless,
Away from books, away from art, the day
    erased, the
lesson done,
Thee fully forth emerging, silent, gazing,
    pondering the
themes thou lovest best,
Night, sleep, death and the stars.

Ah, good-evening. It's the two of them again,
    face to face,
he and his lamp. How he loves that lamp,
    though he may seem
aloof and self-satisfied—loves it not only
because it serves him, but also and especially
because it justifies his attentions;—fragile relic
of ancient Greek lamps, it gathers about it
memories and delicate insects of night; it
    smoothes away
the wrinkles of old age, heightens the brow,
magnifies the shadows of young bodies; covers
with a kindly glow the whiteness of
    blank paper
or the smuggled crimson of poems—and when
at daybreak, its light pales and is merged
with the rose tint of day, with the rumble of
    the first
storefront going up, the first handcarts
    and fruitsellers—
it becomes a palpable image of his
    own wakefulness,

136 and it becomes a bridge of glass that connects
     the glass of his spectacles to the glass of
          the lamp,
     then to the panes of glass in the window, and
          from there
     to the world beyond: a glass bridge that
          holds him
     suspended over the city, and *in* the city—joining
     now of his own free will, the night and the day.

     Translated from the Greek by Martin McKinsey

BERNARD SPENCER

Over the mountains a plane bumbles in;
down in the city a watchman's iron-topped stick
bounces and rings on the pavement.
     Late returners
must be waiting now, by me unseen

To enter shadowed doorways. A dog's pitched
barking flakes and flakes away at the sky.
Sounds and night-sounds, no more; but then
     I catch
my lamp burn fiercer like a thing bewitched,

Table and chairs expectant like a play:
and—if that Unknown, Demon, what you will
stalks on the scene—must live with sounds
     and echoes,
be damned the call to sleep, the needs of day,

Love a dark city; then for some bare bones
of motive, strange perhaps to beast or traveller,
with all I am and all that I have been
sweat the night into words, as who cracks stones.

Gift of the Poem
STÉPHANE MALLARMÉ

I bring you the offspring of an Idumæan night!
Dark, with pale and bleeding wing, plumeless.
Through the casement burnished with incense
    and gold,
Past the frozen panes still bleak, alas!
Dawn burst upon the angel lamp.
Palms! and when it discovered this relic
To this father attempting an inimical smile,
Blue and barren the solitude shuddered.
O cradle-singer, with your child and
    the innocence
Of your cold feet, welcome a horrible birth:
And your voice reminiscent of viol and clavecin,
Will you press with faded finger the breast
Whence woman in sibylline whiteness flows
For lips in the air of the virgin azure famished?

Translated from the French by Kate Flores

WALLACE STEVENS

In the moonlight
I met Berserk,
In the moonlight
On the bushy plain.
Oh; sharp he was
As the sleepless!

And, "Why are you red
In this milky blue?"
I said.
"Why sun-colored,
As if awake
In the midst of sleep?"

"You that wander,"
So he said,
"On the bushy plain,
Forget so soon.
But I set my traps
In the midst of dreams."
I knew from this

That the blue ground
Was full of blocks
And blocking steel.
I knew the dread
Of the bushy plain,
And the beauty
Of the moonlight
Falling there,
Falling
As sleep falls
In the innocent air.

KAGA NO CHIYO

While I was musing on my theme,
Repeating "cuckoo," day has dawned.

Translated from the Japanese by Asatarō Miyamori

Astronomies and slangs to find you, dear

JOHN BERRYMAN

Astronomies and slangs to find you, dear,
Star, art-breath, crowner, conscience! and
    to chart
For kids unborn your distal beauty, part
On part that startles, till you blaze more clear
And witching than your sister Venus here
To a late age can, though her senior start
Is my new insomnia,—swift sleepless art
To draw you even . . and to draw you near.

I prod our English: cough me up a word,
Slip me an epithet will justify
My daring fondle, fumble of far fire
Crackling nearby, unreasonable as a surd,
A flash of light, an insight: I am the shy
Vehicle of your cadmium shine . . your choir.

6

Tonight—I am alone in the night,
a homeless and sleepless nun!
Tonight I hold all the keys to this
the only capital city

and lack of sleep guides me on my path.
You are so lovely, my dusky Kremlin!
Tonight I put my lips to the breast
of the whole round and warring earth.

Now I feel hair—like fur—standing on end:
the stifling wind blows straight into my soul.
Tonight I feel compassion for everyone,
those who are pitied, along with those who
    are kissed.

9

Who sleeps at night? No one is sleeping.
In the cradle a child is screaming.
An old man sits over his death, and anyone

young enough talks to his love, breathes
into her lips, looks into her eyes.

Once asleep—who knows if we'll wake again?
We have time, we have time, we have time
    to sleep!
From house to house the sharp-eyed
watchman goes with his pink lantern
and over the pillow scatters the rattle
of his loud clapper, rumbling.

Don't sleep! Be firm! Listen, the alternative
is—everlasting sleep. Your—everlasting house!

        10
Here's another window
with more sleepless people!
Perhaps—drinking wine or
perhaps only sitting,
or maybe two lovers are
unable to part hands.
Every house has
a window like this.
A window at night: cries

of meeting or leaving.
Perhaps—there are many lights,
perhaps—only three candles.
But there is no peace in
my mind anywhere, for
in my house also, these
things are beginning:

Pray for the wakeful house,
friend, and the lit window.

Translated from the Russian by Elaine Feinstein

My night awake (FROM *The Speed of Darkness*)

MURIEL RUKEYSER

XIII
My night awake
staring at the broad rough jewel
the copper roof across the way
thinking of the poet
yet unborn in this dark
who will be the throat of these hours.
No.   Of those hours.
Who will speak these days,
if not I,
if not you?

RICHARD FROST

> *I heard a whipporwill and a dog crying*
> *about somebody who was going to die.*
> —*Huckleberry Finn*

He clicks off the reading lamp, and it is
    almost morning.
Already the crows are calling and answering,
making their own perfect sense, and the sun
is steadily, imperceptibly, climbing the east hills
to wash away the dark night of words,
the ancient litanies of pain and death
scarcely interrupted by the occasional cry
of a neighbor's chained dog or a nearby owl.
Soon it will be safe, for the world will
    step again
into its garments, and light will seek out
every corner, each black universal truth
that haunts him. Has, how long? The day
    will rise
to its obscure bright work, and he can sleep.

John Berryman (1914–1972), American poet, gained critical attention as a "confessional poet" with the publication of his third book, *Homage to Mistress Bradstreet.* Ten years later, *Dream Songs* won the Pulitzer Prize. Berryman committed suicide by jumping into the Mississippi River.

Elizabeth Bishop (1911–1979), American poet, traveled much of her life, living in many parts of the world before finally settling in Brazil. When she reissued her first book of poems, *North and South*, alongside her second, *A Cold Spring*, the double volume won the Pulitzer Prize. Her *Complete Poems* won the National Book Award.

Louise Bogan (1897–1970), American poet, wrote most of the poetry reviews for the *New Yorker* for many years. Originally from Maine, she gained a reputation, both as a poet and a critic, of being unflinchingly blunt and non-partisan.

Emily Brontë (1818–1848), English poet, best known for her novel *Wuthering Heights*, lived out her life on the North Yorkshire moors in her family home. Before her untimely death, she wrote intense and powerful poems charged with other-worldly mysticism.

Cao Bá Quát (1809–1853), Vietnamese poet, was born near

Hanoi. Constantly at odds with authorities, he launched a peasant rebellion in 1853; he was either killed in battle or captured and put to death. Many of his poems were lost due to official reprisals, but some 1,400 (mostly in Chinese) have been recovered.

Nina Cassian (1924—), Romanian poet, is a translator and classical composer. In 1985 her verses mocking the Ceauşescu regime were discovered, and she was marked for execution. At the time, however, she was visiting friends in New York and was thus able to apply for political asylum in the United States, where she has since remained.

Samuel Taylor Coleridge (1772–1834), English poet, published *Lyrical Ballads*, the revolutionary keystone of Romanticism, with William Wordsworth in 1798. Addicted to opium, Coleridge largely abandoned poetry by his early thirties but remained a crucial inspiration to the Romantic movement in English poetry.

Tristan Corbière (1845–1875), French poet, who wrote much of his poetry while living in isolation in England, came to be considered a preeminent Symbolist poet only after his death. His sole publication prior to his early death was his magnum opus, *The Jaundiced Loves*.

Stephen Cushman (1956—), American poet, is the author of a poetry collection, *Blue Pajamas*, as well as two critical

books, *Fictions of Form in American Poetry* and *William Carlos*
Williams and the Meanings of Measure.

Emily Dickinson (1830–1886), American poet, lived largely in
isolation in Amherst, Massachusetts, leaving little record
of a public life. Her oeuvre, almost two thousand
poems, remained mostly unpublished during her life-
time, though she was posthumously vaulted to extraor-
dinary fame for her original, lapidary verse.

Rita Dove (1952—   ), American poet, served as Poet Laureate
of the United States from 1993 to 1995. Among her many
books of poetry, *Thomas and Beulah* won the Pulitzer Prize.
Dove is also the author of a short story collection, a
novel, a verse drama, and a collection of essays. Her long
list of honors includes the Charles Frankel Prize, a na-
tional Medal in the Humanities from the White House.

Cornelius Eady (1954—   ), American poet, is the author of
five poetry collections. His second book, *Victims of the
Latest Dance Craze*, won the Lamont Poetry Prize. He
currently lives and writes in New York City.

Gunnar Ekelöf (1907–1968), Swedish poet, has been called
"the most difficult of the great Swedish poets,"
yet he has a wide readership both in Sweden and inter-
nationally as a poet, translator, and essayist. His poems
have been translated into English by such poets as
Muriel Rukeyser, Robert Bly, and W. H. Auden.

Richard Frost (1929—   ), American poet, is the author of several poetry collections, including his most recent, *Neighbor Blood*. His poems have appeared in the *Georgia Review*, the *North American Review*, *Seneca Review*, and elsewhere.

Robert Frost (1874–1963), American poet, frustrated with his inability to publish in the United States, moved to England, where he successfully published his first two volumes of poetry. On returning to America, he quickly secured his reputation and went on to publish numerous books of verse, which won him four Pulitzer Prizes. Though born in San Francisco, New England informs most of his poetry.

Dana Gioia (1950—   ), American poet, was born in Los Angeles. In addition to publishing his own poems, and translating and anthologizing Italian poetry, he has worked as a business executive in New York from 1977 to 1996. His respected essays on the New Formalism place him at the front of that movement, and he is well known for his acclaimed tract, "Can Poetry Matter?"

Louise Glück (1943—   ), American poet, lives in Vermont. She is the author of eight books of poems and a collection of essays. Her many awards include the Pulitzer Prize and the National Book Critics Circle Award for Poetry.

Robert Hayden (1913–1980), American poet and a native of
Detroit, is the author of several books of poems, for
which he received numerous awards, including the
Grand Prize for Poetry at the First World Festival of
Negro Arts. He was a member of the Academy of
American Poets and served two terms as poetry consul-
tant to the Library of Congress.

Gerard Manley Hopkins (1844–1889), English poet, was born
near London, converted to Catholicism in 1866, and
entered the Jesuit order two years later. Having burned
his earlier verse as too worldly, Hopkins began, after a
seven-year poetic silence, to craft his highly alliterative,
syntactically complex, and unconventional verse. His
poetry gained immediate fame upon its publication
twenty-nine years after his death.

Mark Jarman (1952—   ), American poet, has received numer-
ous awards for his poetry collections, including the
Joseph Henry Jackson award. His most recent collection
is *Questions for Ecclesiastes*.

Richard Jones (1953—   ), American poet, is cofounder and
editor of *Poetry East*. The author of several collections
of verse, Jones has also edited a number of critical
anthologies, including *Poetry and Politics*.

Donald Justice (1925—   ), American poet, considered one of
the preeminent American lyric poets of his generation,

was born and raised in Miami. He is the author of more than six books of poems, including his *Selected Poems*, which received the Pulitzer Prize. He is also a noted pianist—having studied with the composer Carl Ruggles while a student at the University of Miami— and painter.

Kaga No Chiyo (1703–1775), Japanese poet, also known as Chiyo-jo (indicating a married woman) and later Chiyo-ni (to show she had become a nun), is one of the most popular and beloved Japanese Haiku poets. Even as a young girl she was able to impress her Haiku master with skillful handling of the most difficult forms and subjects.

John Keats (1795–1821), English poet, was apprenticed at age fifteen to a surgeon and later entered a London hospital as a medical student, a career he soon abandoned to pursue a life of poetry. With few exceptions, most of his mature work was produced in a single year. He died prematurely of tuberculosis.

Weldon Kees (1914–1955), American poet, originally known for his stories, turned midway in his brief writing career to poetry. Kees eventually became art editor for *The Nation*, where he was highly involved in promoting the avant-guarde movement. A native Nebraskan, Kees spent most of his adult life in New York.

Jane Kenyon (1947–1995), American poet, is the author of five collections of poetry and a translator of the Russian poet Anna Akhmatova. Kenyon lived and worked with her husband, the poet Donald Hall, in New Hampshire until her untimely death from cancer.

King James Bible [The Book of Job], a translation of the Bible from the Latin Vulgate, ordered by King James I of England in 1604 and completed in 1611, became the standard Bible in Anglican communion. Considered a masterpiece of translation, this Bible has greatly influenced English literature. The Book of Job, believed to be based on ancient Semitic folktales, probes the depth of faith and the meaning of suffering. Scholars' estimations of its time of composition vary, with some positing a date as early as 2100–1550 B.C., and others suggesting c. 550 B.C.

Melissa Kirsch (1974—   ), American poet, is a recent graduate of the MFA Program at New York University. She lives and writes in New York City.

Yusef Komunyakaa (1947—   ), American poet, is a native of Louisiana. He received the Pulitzer prize for *Neon Vernacular* (1993), which was also nominated for the Los Angeles Times Book Prize in poetry the same year.

Louise Labé (1522–1566), French poet, presided over a salon attended by the most learned men of her day. Her poems are notable for their passion and honesty. In 1555 she produced her one publication and magnum opus, *The Debate and Folly of Love.*

Lalla (1320–1392), Indian poet, was a fourteenth-century North Indian mystic famous for wandering, singing, and dancing naked throughout medieval Kashmir. Little is known about her other than what comes through her poetry and what has been preserved through oral lore and tradition.

Philip Larkin (1922–1985), British poet, born in Coventry, worked as a university librarian for most of his life. He wrote two novels as well as perceptive reviews of poetry and jazz. A year before his death, he was offered the Poet Laureateship of England but turned it down.

H. Leivick (1888–1962), Belorussian poet, was born in a remote town in Belorussia to a poor family of nine children. In 1906 he was arrested for having joined the Bund, the underground Jewish social-democratic party, and sentenced to hard labor followed by exile in Siberia. Fortunately, friends in America helped him to escape to the United States, where, while working as a wall-paper hanger and, later, as an editor, he became a renowned figure of Yiddish poetry and drama.

Henry Wadsworth Longfellow (1807–1882), American poet,

receiving early popular acclaim, traveled to Europe for
several years before returning to teach at Harvard. There
he wrote his famous longer poems out of an overtly
American mythology. "The Cross of Snow," written for
his wife who died in a fire, was found in his portfolio
after his death.

Federico García Lorca (1898–1936), Spanish poet, was the son
of a Granadan sugar plantation-owning family. He left
his law studies to pursue the literary life in Madrid,
where he befriended Salvador Dali and the filmmaker
Luis Buñuel. A leading poet and playwright of his day,
he was shot by the Fascists in 1936.

Stéphane Mallarmé (1842–1898), French poet, famous for his
salon and coterie, was not only a leading Symbolist poet
but their primary defender and theoretician. His collect-
ed poems are a slender volume, well-wrought and grace-
fully elliptical.

Osip Mandelstam (1891–1938), Russian poet, produced two
collections of verse during his life. Both *Stone* and *Tristia*
are thought to be models of Acmeism, a Russian move-
ment that advocated concision of language and
unadorned images. Having openly opposed the Soviet
regime, he was arrested in the purges of the 1930s and is
believed to have died in a concentration camp.

Stephen Margulies (1948—   ), American poet, is the Curator of Works on Paper at the Bayly Art Museum of the University of Virginia.

Meleagros (c. first century B.C.), Greek poet, also known as Meleager of Gadara, wrote mainly brief elegies dealing with love and death. A number of his epigrams can be found in the *Greek Anthology*.

Herman Melville (1819–1891), American poet, is best known for his prose, especially the novel *Moby Dick*. His two most noted poetic works are *Battle-Pieces and Aspects of the War*, a group of elegiac Civil War poems, and *Clarel: A Poem and Pilgrimage to the Holy Land*, a long poem concerning a young theology student's struggle with faith.

Robert Mezey (1935—   ), American poet, is the author of many books and translations, and has garnered a number of important literary prizes, including the Lamont Poetry Award.

Mirabai (c. 1498–1550), Indian poet, was a Rajput princess who, rather than fling herself onto her husband's funeral pyre as custom demanded, is reputed to have said, "Take these husbands who wither and die and feed them to your kitchen fires," before leaving the palace to become a wandering mendicant. A devotee of Krishna, she was a key figure in the influential bhakti movement, which rejected the dogma of caste and creed to pursue direct union with God. Her songs were transmitted through popular oral tradition and recorded centuries later.

Debra Nystrom (1954—), American poet, is the author of *A Quarter Turn*, a collection of poems. Her work has appeared in such journals as *Ploughshares* and the *American Poetry Review*. She oversees the publication of the literary journal *Meridian*.

Joyce Carol Oates (1938—), American poet, is a prolific writer well known for her powerful, provocative novels and essays, as well as poetry. She is coeditor of *Ontario Review*.

Mary Oliver (1935—), American poet, born in Ohio, is a writer whose work blends rhetorical innovation and vision with a passionate relationship to nature. Oliver is the author of many books of poetry; among them, *American Primitive* earned her a Pulitzer prize, and *New and Selected Poems* won a National Book Award.

Gregory Orr (1947—), American poet, is the author of nine books of poetry and criticism. He serves as Poetry Consultant for the *Virginia Quarterly Review*.

Patumaṉār (dates unknown), Indian poet, wrote in the flourishing period of Tamil literature (100 B.C.–250 A.D.). There is little historical record of his life; out of a presumably much larger body of poems, only six have survived.

Petrarch (1304–1374), Italian poet, born Francesco Petrarca, was one of the most famous and widely imitated poets of the Middle Ages, and is considered one of the heralds of the Italian Renaissance.

Sylvia Plath (1932–1963), American poet, born in Boston, had a brief, brilliant career as a poet before her suicide. The poems written between 1960 and her death exhibit a particularly desperate and original genius.

Alexander Pushkin (1799–1837), Russian poet, attained literary fame at a very young age and went on to publish successfully in every major genre. A stellar figure of Russian literature, he is considered to have single-handedly constructed the beginnings of a classical literature for that country.

Salvatore Quasimodo (1901–1968), Italian poet, gained an international following when he received the Nobel Prize for Literature in 1959. Quasimodo was cited by the Nobel Prize Committee for his "lyrical poetry which with classical fire expresses the tragic experience of our time."

Arthur Rimbaud (1854–1891), French poet, ran away from home at age fifteen, traveling to Paris to pursue a life of debauchery which he hoped would accelerate his development into a mystical seer and poet. The Symbolists were quick to place his work in the public sphere. All of his poetry was written before the age of thirty, at which time he left for Africa and the Middle East to become a gunrunner and slave trader.

Yannis Ritsos (1909–1990), Greek poet, was an avid Communist persecuted by the Fascists when they took over Greece in 1936. His books were burned and remained banned until 1954. Despite periods of exile, imprisonment, and bouts of tuberculosis, Ritsos managed to produce more than a hundred books of poetry, drama, and translation.

Dante Gabriel Rossetti (1828–1882), English poet, was the key founder of the Pre-Raphaelite Brotherhood, from which he later turned away in favor of the Aestheticism and Decadence movements. Rossetti was also an important painter and translator.

Muriel Rukeyser (1913–1980), American poet, was born in New York City. Rukeyser, who also translated poetry and wrote biographies and children's books, has been a key influence in the evolution of contemporary women's poetry.

Ryōkan (c. 1758–1831), Japanese poet, was born in a remote province of Japan to a prosperous literary family. In 1777 he became a Buddhist monk.

Umberto Saba (1883–1957), Italian poet, was an antiquarian bookseller in Trièste. On coming into power, the Fascists were quick to persecute Saba because of his Jewish origins, and it was only after World War II that he became known as one of the outstanding Italian literary figures of his day.

Sappho (b. 612 B.C.), Greek poet, was a native of Lesbos, where, except for a brief period of years spent in Sicily, she remained throughout her life. She led a school for young girls, famous in its day, primarily devoted to the study of music and poetry. Hailed by classical writers as "The Tenth Muse," her work survives only in fragmentary form.

Robert Schultz (1951—), American poet, is the author of a novel, *The Madhouse Nudes*, and two poetry collections.

William Shakespeare (1564–1616), English poet, was an actor, shareholder, and principal playwright at the most sought-after theater company of his day. His many sonnets, like his plays, went uncollected during his life. Rather, they were circulated in manuscript form among intimate friends, receiving public audience only posthumously.

Sir Philip Sidney (1554–1586), English poet, was a prominent courtier in the court of Queen Elizabeth, from which he was eventually banished. In exile, he began his famous critical work, *Defense of Poetry*, the pastoral romance *Arcadia*, as well as *Astrophel and Stella*, the first sonnet sequence in English. He died in battle at age thirty-two, fighting for Protestantism.

Charles Simic (1938—   ), American poet, born in Yugoslavia, has won many awards for his books of poetry and translations, among them, the Pulitzer Prize for *The World Doesn't End*, a P.E.N. Translation Prize, and a MacArthur Foundation Fellowship.

R. T. Smith (1947—   ), American poet, is editor of the literary journal *Shenandoah*. Among his several books are the collections *The Cardinal Heart* and *Trespasser*.

Bernard Spencer (1909–1963), English poet, born in Madras, India, and educated in England, left behind when he died a small but remarkable body of poetry. His *Collected Poems* totals only ninety-six pages.

Wallace Stevens (1879–1955), American poet, was a lawyer and vice president of the Hartford Accident and Indemnity Co. and lived a life entirely apart from literary circles. Though he published in *Poetry* as early as 1914, it was not until 1931 that his first book appeared. It was only when he won the Pulitzer Prize in 1954 that he achieved the widespread critical acclaim that has established him as one of the great American poets of the twentieth century.

Adrien Stoutenburg (1916–1982), American poet, was born in Minnesota. She won a Lamont Poetry Award for *Heroes, Advise Us*. Stoutenburg also wrote short stories and young adult fiction.

Mark Strand (1934—   ), American poet, was born in Canada and originally studied painting at Yale before turning to poetry. He has published many books of poems noted for their elegiac, deeply inward sense of language.

Trần Thái-tông, King (1218–1277), Vietnamese poet, rose from the humble background of a Vietnamese fisherman's family to found the Tran dynasty in 1225. He was a devout Buddhist who wrote expertly on his faith.

Marina Tsvetaeva (1892–1941), Russian poet, spent most of her adult life in poverty. When, against her will, she emigrated to Paris in the 1920s, she was already recognized as one of the great Russian poets of this century. On returning to Russia in 1941, feeling isolated and marginalized despite her fame, she took her own life.

Tu Fu (712–770 A.D.), Chinese poet, was born into a genteel literary family in China. A genius of Chinese formal invention, he remained virtually anonymous during his lifetime, his some 1,500 surviving poems nearly forgotten for three hundred years.

Utitia'q's Song [Inuit] (anonymous), is a traditional Inuit "song poem," adapted by Brian Swann from a version set down by Franz Boas in the *Journal of American Folklore* in 1894. Swann writes: "Utitia'q went adrift on the ice while sealing and only reached shore after a week of hardship."

Ellen Bryant Voigt (1943—   ), American poet, born and raised in Virginia, now lives in Vermont. She is the author of five books of poetry and has contributed to, and edited, numerous others.

Walt Whitman (1819–1892), American poet, was fired from his post with the Department of the Interior for having authored the "scandalous" *Leaves of Grass*. Whitman thought of himself as the "bard of democracy," employing long, organic lines and open forms to create a literary voice that made him an immense figure in American letters even by the time of his own death.

Charles Wright (1935—   ), American poet, translator, and essayist, is the winner of the Pulitzer Prize for his collection *Black Zodiac*. His many other awards include the National Book Award, an Ingram Merrill Fellowship, and the Lenore Marshall poetry prize.

by Cornelius Eady. Copyright © 1991 by Cornelius   169
Eady. Reprinted by permission of Carnegie-Mellon
University Press.

Gunnar Ekelöf: "The Moon." From *Friends, You Drank Some
Darkness*, edited and translated by Robert Bly. Reprinted
by permission of the translator.

Richard Frost: "The Night Person." Copyright © 1998 by *The
Gettysburg Review* (vol. 11, no. 3). Reprinted by permission
of the editors of *The Gettysburg Review*.

Robert Frost: "Acquainted with the Night." From *The Poetry of
Robert Frost* by Robert Frost. Edited by Edward Connery
Lathem. Copyright 1928, © 1969 by Henry Holt &
Company, © 1956 by Robert Frost. Reprinted by per-
mission of Henry Holt & Company, Inc., the Estate
of Robert Frost, and Jonathan Cape, Publisher.

Louise Glück: "Moonless Night." From *Meadowlands* by
Louise Glück. Copyright © 1996 by Louise Glück.
Reprinted by permission of The Ecco Press.

Dana Gioia: "Insomnia." From *Daily Horoscope* by Dana
Gioia. Copyright © 1986 by Dana Gioia. Reprinted
with the permission of Graywolf Press, Saint Paul,
Minnesota.

Robert Hayden: "The Broken Dark." From *Collected Poems of
Robert Hayden* by Robert Hayden. Edited by Frederick
Glaysher. Copyright © 1970 by Robert Hayden.

Melissa Kirsch: "Sleep's Underside." Reprinted by permission   171
  of the author.

Yusef Komunyakaa: "When Loneliness Is a Man." From *Neon
  Vernacular* by Yusef Komunyakaa. Copyright © 1993 by
  Yusef Komunyakaa. Reprinted by permission of Wes-
  leyan University Press.

Louise Labé: "Bright Venus, who across the heavens stray."
  Sonnet 5 from *Sonnets* by Louise Labé. Translated by
  Graham Dunstan Martin. Copyright © 1972 by The
  Edinburgh Bilingual Library. Reprinted by permission
  of Edinburgh University Press.

Lalla: "At the end of a crazy-moon night." From *Naked Song*
  by Lalla. Translated by Coleman Barks. Copyright ©
  1992. Reprinted by permission of the translator.

Philip Larkin: "Aubade." From *Collected Poems* by Philip
  Larkin. Copyright © 1988, 1989 by the Estate of Philip
  Larkin. Reprinted by permission of Farrar, Straus and
  Giroux, Inc., and of Faber and Faber Ltd.

H. Leivick: "Lament at Night." Translated by Marie Syrkin
  from *A Treasury of Yiddish Poetry*, edited by Irving Howe
  and Eliezer Greenberg. Copyright © 1969 by Schocken
  Books.

Federico García Lorca: "Ballad of One Doomed to Die." From
  The Selected Poems of Federico García Lorca by Federico García
  Lorca. Translated by Langston Hughes. Copyright ©

Reprinted with permission of Hohm Press, Prescott,
Arizona.

Debra Nystrom: "Insomnia." From *A Quarter Turn* by Debra
Nystrom. Copyright © 1991 by Debra Nystrom.
Reprinted with permission of Sheep Meadow Press.

Joyce Carol Oates: "Insomnia." From *Tenderness* by Joyce Carol
Oates. Copyright © 1996 by The Ontario Review Press,
Inc. Reprinted with permission of The Ontario Review
Press, Inc.

Mary Oliver: "White Night." From *American Primitive* by
Mary Oliver. Copyright © 1982 by Mary Oliver. "White
Night" first appeared in *Virginia Quarterly Review*. Reprint-
ed by permission of Little, Brown and Company.

Gregory Orr: "Insomnia Song." Reprinted by permission of
the author.

Patumanār: "What She Said." From *The Interior Landscape*,
edited and translated by A. K. Ramanujan. Copyright
© 1967 by Indiana University Press.

Petrarch: [For whatever animals dwell on earth] Poem no. 22
from *Petrarch's Lyric Poems* by Petrarch. Edited and trans-
lated by Robert M. Durling. Copyright © 1976 by
Robert Durling. Reprinted by permission of Harvard
University Press, Cambridge, Mass.

Sylvia Plath: "Insomniac." From *Crossing the Water* by Sylvia
Plath. Copyright © 1965 by Ted Hughes. Copyright

174   Renewed. Reprinted by permission of HarperCollins
      Publishers, Inc., and of Faber and Faber Ltd.

Alexander Pushkin: "Lines Written at Night During Insom-
nia." From *The Bronze Horseman* by Alexander Pushkin.
Translated by D. M. Thomas. Copyright © 1982 by The
Viking Press. Reprinted by permission of John Johnson
(Author's Agent) Ltd.

Salvatore Quasimodo: "Insomnia." From *The Selected Writings of
Salvatore Quasimodo* by Salvatore Quasimodo. Translated
by Allen Mandelbaum. Copyright © 1954, 1960 by
Minerva Press.

Arthur Rimbaud: "Night of Hell." From *A Season in Hell &
The Drunken Boat* by Arthur Rimbaud. Translated by
Louise Varese. Copyright © 1961 by New Directions
Publishing Corp. Reprinted by permission of New
Directions Publishing Corp.

Yannis Ritsos: "His Lamp Near Daybreak." First published in
Greek by Kedros Editions (1963). Translated by Martin
McKinsey. Reprinted by permission of the translator.

Muriel Rukeyser: "Nevertheless the moon" and "My
night awake." From *The Collected Poems of Muriel
Rukeyser*.

Ryōkan: Sections from "Winter." From *One Robe, One Bowl*
by Ryōkan. Translated by John Stevens. Copyright ©
1977 by Weatherhill. Reprinted by permission.